You may learn how to draw a range of creatures with this book. The first Illustration is not required to be read initially. Whichever you want, pick. Once you've made a decision, implement it using the steps outlined. Sketch out the first action with extreme care and lightness. The easiest stage, though, needs to be completed with the utmost care. The second step is added immediately after the first, also delicately. The third step is drawn directly over the first and second steps. Achieve the final stage in this manner.

It may seem unusual to ask you to take more care when you are drawing the initial phases, which seem to be the simplest, but these are the most crucial because a thoughtless error at the start could ruin the entire picture in the end. Watch the lines and the gaps between the lines as you sketch out each step to ensure accuracy. You might want to push the previous stages with a kneaded eraser to make them lighter after each step (available at art supply stores).

After you're done, you might want to go back and recreate the last step in India ink using a fine brush or pen. Use the kneaded eraser to remove the pencil lines when the ink has dried.

How to
Draw a
Quail

For the quail's first portion of the body, draw a large circle as a guide. To represent the circle's height and width, first make four tiny markings, then draw curving lines to link them. Start out with a light hand when sketching so that mistakes are simple to fix. However, the circle need not be flawless. It is merely a guide. Trace the circumference of a glass, a cup, or any other object with a round edge if you do want a flawless circle.

To serve as a guide for the bird's head, draw another circle on the top, right side. The size of this circle should be roughly one-fifth that of the first. You shouldn't draw the head too close to the body because quails have lengthy necks.

Draw a curving horizontal line inside the head. You can later position the quail's facial characteristics using this building line.

Draw a line that resembles a greater-than symbol (>) on the right side of the head to serve as a guide for the quail's beak.

Draw two lines that connect the head to the body to create the guide for the quail's neck. Curve the lines to make the bird's neck more organic and less stiff.

Draw a big, wide arc on the lower, left side of the first circle as a guide for the bottom half of the quail's body. The combined shape of the arc and the first circle should be similar to an egg.

To serve as a reference point for the quail's legs, draw a few brief, straight lines underneath the body.

Draw another arc on the lower, left side of the body as a guide for the quail's tail. This arc should be long and narrower than the arc for the body.

For the quail's eye, lightly draw a little circle inside the head. Place the items using the construction line as a reference. Darken the circle after the bird's eye is the proper size and position.

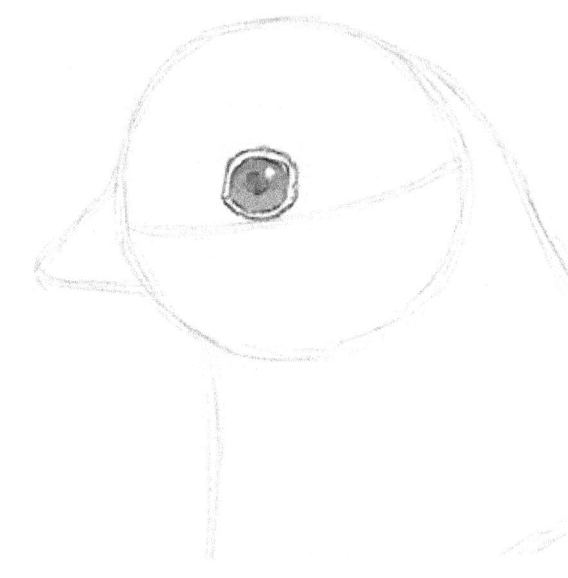

Draw the quail's beak using the angled line on the right side of the head as a reference. To build the top of the beak, make the line more curved while still adhering to the main guideline. Now outline the aperture of the beak as a curved line with a point inside the bird's head. To build the bottom of the beak, create a line that is more curved while still adhering to the bottom portion of the guide. Create the feathery base of the beak on the left side with a series of swift, brief strokes.

Use the intial circle and connecting lines as guides to draw the shape of the head. Use quick, short strokes as you follow the outer edge of the guides to create the shape of the head. Use quick, short strokes under the beak to create the quail's feathery throat.

Create a path for the feathers on the quail's head by lightly drawing a curving line. Create the texture of the feathers by making rapid, brief strokes that trace the route of the line you just drew. The plume, or crown of feathers, should droop and nearly touch the top of the beak. The quail's plume should be broad and curved at the tip, with a narrow base.

Use a succession of short, rapid strokes to create the markings on the quail's head. First, make two curving lines over the eye in a series of rapid, short strokes. Next, make a tiny line between the beak and the bird's lower, right eye.

Draw another series of curving lines, this time from the throat to the eye, in rapid, short strokes.

Near the top of the body's form, trace the contour of the quail's folded wing. Essentially, the folded wing is a series of shorter curved lines extending over the body. Instead of being one continuous line, the folded wing's line should be broken up.

Draw the legs using the lines underneath the body as a guide. The feathery foundation should be drawn first as a curved line at the top. Then, as you follow the directions' instructions, make the bird's leg, foot, and toe shapes thicker. Draw a curled, spike-like shape for the claws on the tips of each toe. Each foot of a quail has three toes facing forward and one toe pointing backward. Only draw what is visible because the toes that point forward will overlap when viewed from this angle.

To draw the other leg in the same manner, use the first leg as a guide. Only depict the portions that are visible from this perspective since the first leg of the quail will cover a significant portion of the leg on the other side.

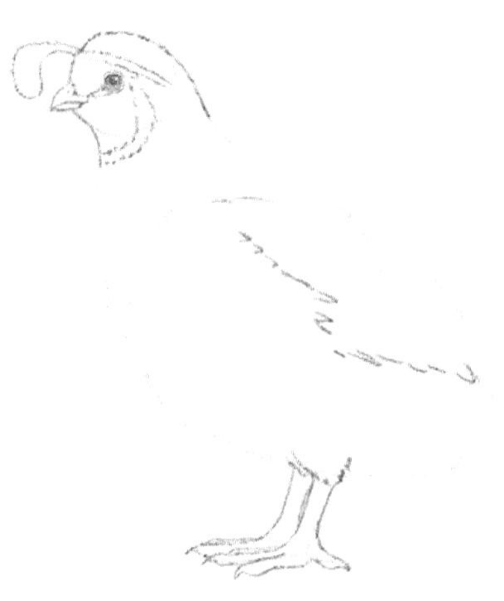

Draw the rest of the body using the basic lines and shapes as your instructions. To make the quail's body, simply darken the guidelines' outer edges. On the left side's lowest portion, use short, swift strokes.

To draw the quail's tail, follow the tiny arc on the bottom, left side of the body. Create the bird's tail by darkening the guide's route and adding a few rapid, brief strokes at the base.

As much of the first guiding lines as you can remove for a cleaner appearance. Don't stress about removing every guide. You can abandon some of them. If you unintentionally removed any lines from your final sketch, redo them.

For more detail, you can add value all over your quail drawing. When shading the group of sagging feathers on the head, use a dark value. On the head, add a dark value as well, but omit the banded design. On the beak, use a tad lighter of a value.

As a guide for the quokka's head, draw a circle near the top of the paper. Make four marks to represent the circle's height and width before drawing it. Then draw curving lines to join the marks together. Start out with a light hand when sketching so that mistakes are simple to fix. Simply trace the outer rim of a coin or a lid if you're having trouble drawing a circle.

As a guide for later placement of the quokka's facial features, draw a curved, horizontal line across the head. Draw a smaller, curved, vertical line for another building guide on the top, right side.

Draw a little circle below the point where the building lines converge to serve as a guide for the quokka's muzzle. Take note of how big this circle is in relation to the head. Avoid making it overly large.

To make the quokka's ears, draw two little arcs on the top of the skull.

Draw a large circle under the head, off to the left, to serve as a guide for the top of the quokka's body. Draw this circle utilizing the four-mark technique as well, beginning with a loose sketch to ensure the proper shape. This circle needs to be roughly twice as big as the prior one. Don't overlap the lines for the shapes because the top of this circular should be behind the head.

Make a mark well below the large circle to add the guidance for the lower part of the quokka's body. To create a large arc, join the little mark to the circle's edges with lengthy, curving lines. The bottom edge should be rather flat, and the left side should be longer than the right.

Make a mark well below the large circle to add the guidance for the lower part of the quokka's body. To create a large arc, join the little mark to the circle's edges with lengthy, curving lines. The bottom edge should be rather flat, and the left side should be longer than the right.

For the quokka's eyes, lightly draw two tiny circles inside the head. Placement guidelines can be found in the first few lines. Darken the shapes once you get the proper size and placement. Because of how the head is oriented, the eye on the left should be a little bit thinner and smaller than the eye on the right. For the eyelids, doodle a few curving lines around the eyes. For some fur, add a few brief strokes above the eyes.

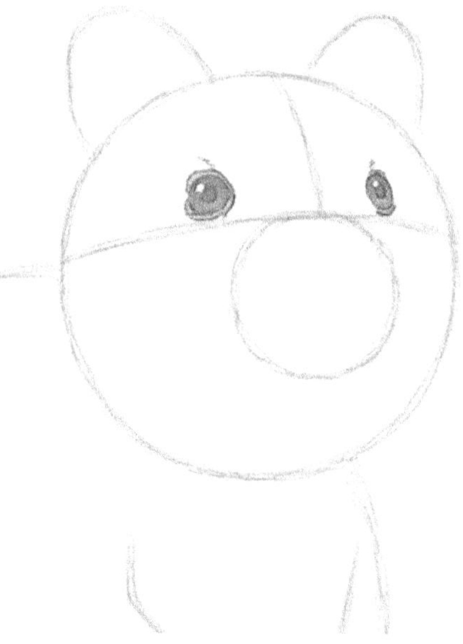

Lightly draw the nose's little circle inside the muzzle. Don't make the shape too small because quokkas have rather large nostrils. Draw it in near to the muzzle's right side. Darken the form once you have the nose's size and placement perfect. The nostrils are made by curving the lines inward as you darken the sides of the nose. Make the bottom of the nose pointed, and in the center, draw a thin line. For fur, add a few brief strokes over the nose.

Lightly draw a line that curves to the left below the nose to represent the beginning of the mouth. For the opposite half of the mouth, draw a second line with a rightward curve. Draw the exterior of the muzzle by adhering to the initial circle's rim. Towards the eye, bend the line. Darken the left side of the mouth upward toward the edge of the circle to create the famous quokka smile. Draw a small line with short strokes behind the mouth to represent the fuzzy chin.

To make the first ear, darken the arc on the top, left side of the head. To give the ear additional structure, add a few curved lines along the inner edge of the arc. For the inside of the ear's fur, make a series of brief strokes within the arc. Draw the opposite ear of the quokka in the same manner, using the arc on the left as a guide. Add strokes inside the arc and make it darker.

To draw the rest of the quokka's head, follow the original circle as a reference. Above the edge of the circle representing the top of the head, draw a line with brief strokes between the ears. Along the sides of the original circle for the hairy head, do a succession of brief strokes. To lengthen the head, draw the bottom portion of the head below the initial circle's rim. To show where the head joins the body, leave a few gaps at the bottom margin. To accentuate the fur, use a few brief strokes inside the quokka's head.

To draw the first arm of the quokka, follow the line inside the large circle to the left. Draw a rough outline of the arm's shape around the course of the guide. As you darken the arm's outline to create the fur, use a succession of little strokes. For the bottom of the hands and digits, use rounded lines. Make a series of small, V-shaped lines for the digits along the bottom of the shape. Draw the other arm in the same manner, using the line on the right as a reference. The bottom V-shaped digits should be added. The contour of the quokka's furry arm is created by drawing tiny strokes all around the guide.

Draw the first leg using the angled line on the lower, left side of the body as a reference. Draw two thin, long shapes for two of the three toes on the right side of the guide line after darkening it. Draw a tiny, curled, triangular shape for the quokka's claws at the end of each toe. Draw a line with tiny strokes that curls upward above the foot to represent the top of the leg. Draw the opposite leg in the same manner, using the line on the right as a guide. For the toes, draw two long, slender curves. Create a little, triangular shape for the toe's claws at the tips of each.

Draw the remainder of the body using the leftover lines and shapes as a reference. Create the body shape of the quokka by darkening the guidelines' outside edges with brief, swift strokes. To give the back more of an arching shape, slightly curve the line on the left as you draw the strokes. Avoid using long strokes since they will make the fur look overly shaggy. To make the bottom of the body narrower, slope the line on the right inward and toward the left side. The top of the right leg is created by drawing a curved line over the foot and along the direction of the guide. On the top portion of the paper, make a series of brief strokes.

As much of the first guiding lines as you can remove for a cleaner appearance. Don't stress about removing every guide. You can abandon some of them. If you unintentionally removed any lines from your final sketch, redo them.

How to Draw a
Rabbit

As a reference point for the rabbit's body, draw a slanted oval.

As a guidance for the rabbit's head, draw an egg-like form above the body.

Draw two intersecting lines inside the head. You can use these as guides to later put the rabbit's face features.

For the rabbit's ears, draw two lengthy arcs on top of the head.

As a reference for the rabbit's feet, draw three lines underneath the body.

Step 6

Draw a circle above the point where the two lines converge to represent the rabbit's eye. For the pupil, add another circle within and shade it.

Draw a circle above the point where the two lines converge to represent the rabbit's eye. For the pupil, add another circle within and shade it.

For further detail, add a few whiskers to the rabbit's muzzle. Draw them in with short, swift strokes.

Refine the rabbit's ears' appearance. Fill them in quickly and briefly, using the initial shape as a guide. To give them a hairy appearance, add more lines within them.

Draw in the remainder of the rabbit's head using the egg shape as a reference once more. To achieve a hairy appearance, keep your strokes short and fast. To add detail, add some lines around the rabbit's eye.

Draw the rabbit's feet in using the lines as guidance. Draw the feet as a huge curve that encircles the guiding line because rabbits have large hind legs. The rabbit's front feet should be drawn using the same technique, but considerably smaller. At the bottom, make a few lines to depict toes.

12

Draw the rest of the rabbit's body, using the oval as a guide, by making fur-representing rapid, short strokes once more. You cannot see the rabbit's tail because it is seated, but you are free to draw one if you choose.

You can either stop here for a rough appearance or try to remove as much of the original guidelines as you can. Concerning removing them all, don't worry. You can abandon some of them.

To give your rabbit drawing more depth and volume, add some shading. When shading, choose the light source's direction so that the shadows follow it. To obtain varying levels of tonal value, alter the pressure you apply to your pencil.

To add more detail, you can increase the value across your bunny drawing. To evoke the appearance of fur, paint the body in short, swift strokes. Using references can help you be as accurate as you can.

As a reference point for the first portion of the sparrow's body, draw a large circle. To represent the circle's height and width, first make four tiny markings, then draw curving lines to link them. Start out with a light hand when sketching so that mistakes are simple to fix. However, the circle need not be flawless. It is merely a guide. Trace the circumference of a glass, a cup, or any other object with a round edge if you do want a flawless circle. Make sure the head and tail of the bird can fit comfortably on the sides.

Draw another circle on the top, right side as a guide for the sparrow's head. Pay attention to the size of this circle in relation to the first one. It should be about one-fourth the size of the first one. Don't draw the circles apart from each other. Their edges should touch.

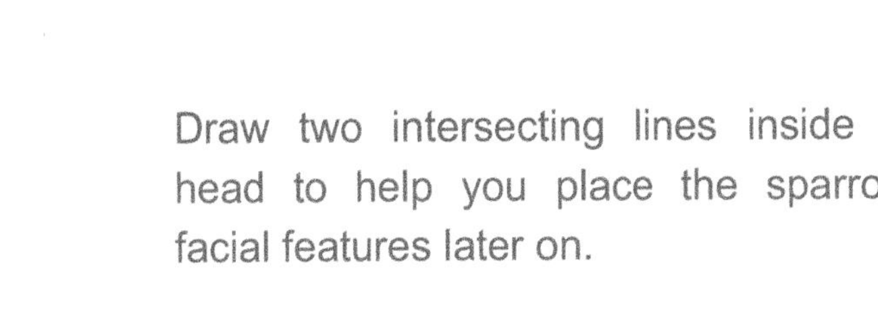

Draw two intersecting lines inside the head to help you place the sparrow's facial features later on.

Draw an angled line on the right side of the head as a guide for the sparrow's beak. The shape of the line should be similar to a greater-than sign (>).

Use a few curved lines around the main circle to finish the shape of the bird's body. First draw two curved lines from the head to the body to form the neck. Then draw a big, wide arc on the lower, left side of the circle for the bottom half of the sparrow's body. The combined shape of the arc and the first circle should be similar to an egg.

Draw a series of lines under the body as guides for the sparrow's legs. First draw a diagonal line, then under it draw a horizontal line. Add another set of similar lines on the right for the leg on the other side.

As a reference for the sparrow's tail, draw a long, thin arc on the lower, left side of the body. To accurately capture the curve of the arc, begin with a simple sketch. Pay close attention to how long the arc is in relation to how big the bird's body is.

Draw a faint circle for the eye within the sparrow's head. Place the eye according to the building lines inside the head. Darken the lines until you have the eye's position and shape perfect. Draw a small, off-center circle inside the eye to depict glare and a larger dot in the center to represent the pupil.

Except for the little circle that stands for glare, cover the inside of the eye. Use a value that is slightly lighter than the pupil to shade the bird's eye. For the naked skin present there, draw a few lines around the eye. The skin around the eyes should be drawn with a series of brief, curving lines.

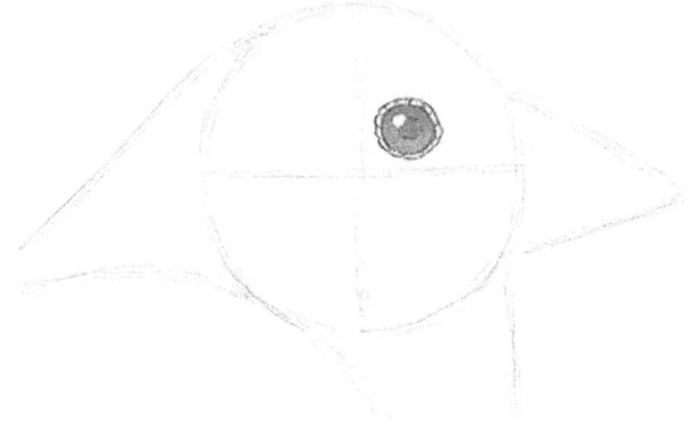

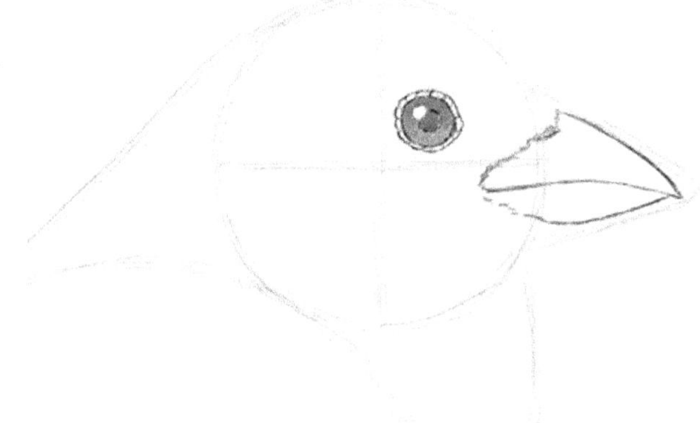

Draw the sparrow's beak using the triangle-like shape on the right side of the head as a guidance. To build the top of the beak, make the line more curved while still adhering to the main guideline. Next, draw a curving line in the middle of the beak that extends inward toward the head.

The fundamental course of the instruction should still be followed, but you should make the line more wavy to produce the bottom of the beak. Make a succession of swift, brief strokes on the left side to create the feathery base of the bird's beak. The beak's base has an angle that is the opposite of the beak's. The form must resemble a less-than symbol ().

The sparrow's head should be drawn using the first circle as a guide. To make the top of the head, darken the line while adhering to the top edge of the circular. To make the back of the head, extend the line in the direction of the left-hand guidance. For the feathery throat of the bird, use short, swift strokes under the beak. For the shape of the neck, add a few rapid, brief strokes within the head as well.

To begin the pattern and color separation of the sparrow, draw a series of lines inside its face. At the base of the beak, draw a curving line that extends to the back of the head. To resemble feathers, the line should be drawn with brief, swift strokes. To the left of the eye, draw a brief, curving line.

Create the second color separation for the sparrow by drawing a longer line behind the eye. Beginning at the neck, this line should curve beneath the eye and end on the left side, close to the rear of the bird's head.

A set of curving lines placed inside the body will be used to represent the top of the bird's wing. Darken the body's left side first. Then draw a couple quick, curving lines down the center. To construct the inner border of the folded wing of the sparrow, bend the line back up toward the head. For the pattern separation, add a few rapid, brief strokes on the upper, right side of the wing.

Use the beginning lines as a reference while you draw the lower portion of the wing. A letter V with a small rightward slant may be seen in the first portion of the sparrow's wing. The second component is the wing's tip, which is composed of numerous lengthy lines that converge at a place. This folded wing's tip should extend to the left, toward the tail guide.

Draw the body's shape using the starting lines as guidance. To make the sparrow's body, simply darken the outer edges of the instructions on the right and bottom.

The sparrow's first foot should be drawn using the lines underneath the body on the left side as a guide. As you follow the directions' lead, thicken the contour of the leg, feet, and toes. On each foot of a sparrow, one toe points backward and three toes point forward. Draw a curled, spike-like shape for the bird's claws on the end of each toe. Only draw what is visible because the toes that point forward will overlap when viewed from this angle.

Draw the other foot of the sparrow using the lines under the body on the right as a reference. As you follow the instructions, make the contour of the leg, foot, and toes thicker. Only draw the portions that are visible because the other leg will cover some of this leg.

To draw the sparrow's tail, follow the thin, long arc on the lower, left side of the body. Just proceed along the guide's path, darkening the lines as you go. To separate the bird's feathers, draw a line at the center of the arc.

To give your sparrow drawing additional depth and volume, add some shading. When shading, choose the light source's direction so that the shadows follow it. To obtain varying levels of tonal value, alter the pressure you apply to your pencil.

Subsequent to your sparrow, add a cast shadow. The bird appears to be grounded as a result of this. For the diffusion of the shadow, place a darker value close to the center and a lighter value around the periphery.

How to Draw a

Cartoon Bunny

For the bunny's eyes, draw two curving lines next to one another. Pay close attention to where the lines are placed. Keep them from being too closely spaced. Create thick lines to resemble eyelashes. The curved lines should resemble a half-circle in shape. Initially, draw these lines very lightly. Darken them once you've achieved the desired placement and shape.

Draw a little circle for the cartoon bunny's irises under each curving line. Close to the rightmost point of the line, the circle on the left should be. The circle on the right ought to be nearer to the curving line's center.

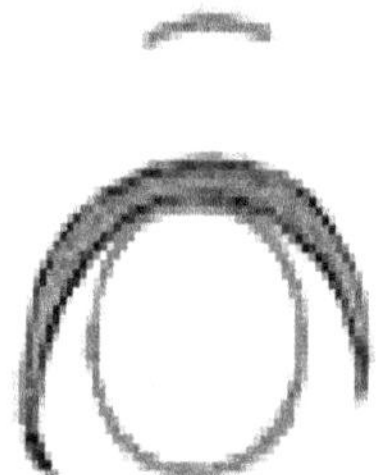

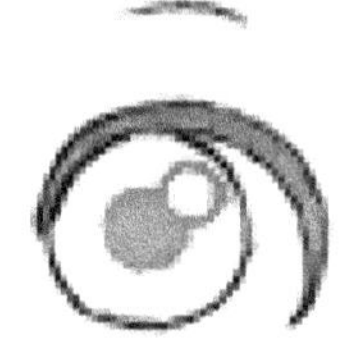

Draw a little circle inside each iris to simulate glare. It should be off to the side. Make a large dot for each pupil in the center of each iris.

Create a tiny triangle for the bunny's nose by drawing it between the eyes and just below them.

Make the bunny's mouth by drawing a little W-shaped line beneath the nose.

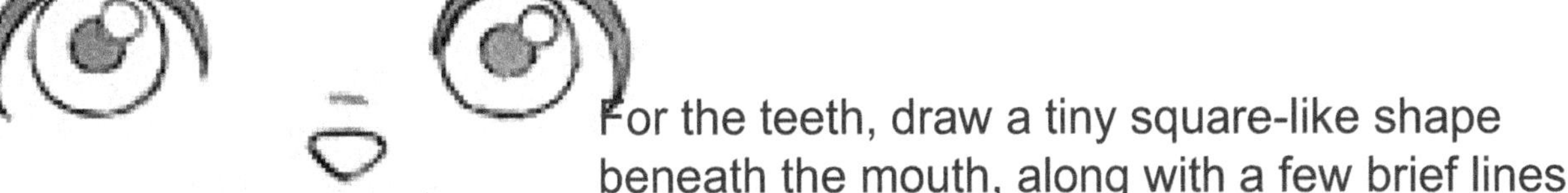

For the teeth, draw a tiny square-like shape beneath the mouth, along with a few brief lines.

By initiial adding a curved vertical line adjacent to the left eye, you may add the cartoon bunny's head. Add a second vertical line to the right, this time farther from the eye. Draw the top half with a curved horizontal line above the eyes, using short, fast strokes to imitate fur

For the bunny's first ear, draw a tall arc on the top, left side of the head that resembles an upside-down letter U. To add more detail, draw a few lines inside the ear.

Draw a quick, curved vertical line on the top, left side of the skull before adding the other ear. Next, draw a longer, curved line on the left side to represent the folded portion of the ear. Use a succession of brief lines to draw the remainder of the bunny's ear behind the folded portion.

For the fur, make rapid, short strokes on either side of the bunny's cheeks. The bottom of the cheeks should be curved such that the end point nearly touches the mouth. Due to the tilt of the head, the right cheek should be wider.

Use a series of rapid, short strokes to draw the chest under the head. The cartoon bunny's chest should have a general form resembling a half-circle.

Draw two brief, vertical lines for the top of the first leg under the chest, close to the right. The foot's bottom will now have a curved line added, and the inside of the toes will have short lines.

Draw the other rabbit leg in a same fashion. Remember to include your toes at the bottom!

Draw a long, curved line for the lower portion of the body, beginning at the lower, right side of the head.

Draw a C-shaped line for the top of the bunny's hind leg to the right of the front foot.

By adding a long, curved line at the bottom, you may add the large foot. On the left side, sketch the toes as brief lines.

Draw a sequence of brief, curving lines in the form of a half-circle to represent the bunny's tail on the lower, right side.

To make the drawing of the cartoon bunny permanent, gently trace over the lines using a pen or marker. After inking, use an eraser to remove all traces of the pencil.

Use colored pencils, markers, or even crayons to add color to your bunny design! To draw a line separating the colors, use brown. Leave the inner of the eyes white and add the lower edge. Now, just the bunny's ears, muzzle, breast, and tail should be light brown. For the nose and inside of the ears, use pink. Color the top portion dark brown and the bottom portion light brown to create a gradient look on the

How to Draw a

Rhino

Make the eyebrow of the charging rhino a short, sloping line. To highlight the thickness of the brow, draw an extra-short line on the left and curve the line's tips.

Draw a curving line for the bottom edge of the eye below the brow. Draw a large dot for the rhino's pupil inside the eye on the left-hand side.

Draw a short, curving line for the horn's base to the lower left of the eye. Draw a long, curved line for the upper side of the rhino's horn at the top of the base. To complete the sharp horn shape, add a last curved line at the bottom.

Draw a long, curved line for the muzzle under the horn. Create the mouth of the rhino by curving the line on the right side up and then down.

Draw a few tiny lines for the nostrils to the left of the mouth. Draw a few more lines for the rhino's bottom lip and chin to the right of the mouth.

For the rhino's jaw, draw a lengthy, curving line on the right side. To the left, draw a long vertical line for the head. For the opposite brow, add a hump in the centre.

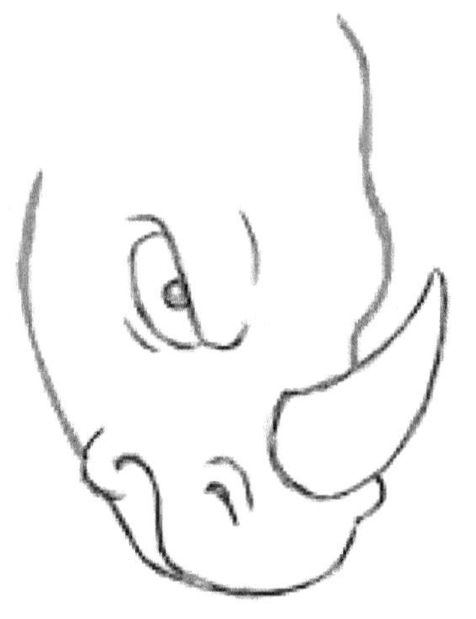

Draw a leaf-like form for the rhino's first ear on the top, right side of the head. For the base of the ear, draw a pair of quick, curving lines at the bottom.

For the rhino's other ear, draw another leaf-like design on the left side.

Lightly draw a long, curved, hilllike line for the rhino's back or hump, starting at the left ear. When the shape is perfect, add a few folds on the left and darken the line. At the bottom, add a few more curved lines for the chest and a second neck crease.

Draw the first segment of the rhino's front leg with three brief, curving lines directly behind the skull.

Draw three shorter lines for the rhino's toes and a curved line for the foot's sole.

Draw a series of curving lines to represent the top of the other front leg at the bottom. The side lines resemble an extremely long letter T. Add a couple of curved lines at the top for creases. These lines shouldn't be too long.

For the lowest portion of the rhino's leg, draw a lengthy, curved line. The sole of this leg needs to be facing backward and bent. Don't drop the curve too low.

Draw a long, sloping line for the rhino's underside to the right of the front leg. Draw another lengthy, curved line for the rump at the top.

Draw the hind leg using a sequence of curving lines on the lower, right side of the torso. The leg should be wide at the top and bottom and narrow in the middle. The leg's top should extend past its bottom. The rhino's toes are shown on the foot by two brief lines.

Draw the other hind leg peeking behind the torso with a few curving lines. Draw a few U-shaped lines on the right side of the torso to represent the rhino's short tail. Draw a succession of little strokes for the brush-like tip at the top of the tail.

To make your design of the charging rhino permanent, carefully trace over the lines with a pen or marker. After inking, use an eraser to remove all traces of the pencil.

Use colored pencils, markers, or even crayons to add color to your rhino drawing! For the body, use gray. Also, add some gray to the horn's base. Black for the tail and pink for the ears. Remember to pause the video so you may sketch at your own leisure.

For the body's front portion of the rooster, draw a circle as a reference. The circle need not be flawless. It is merely a guide. Draw the rooster's head and long tail with enough room on the top right and left.

To complete the body guide for the rooster, draw an arc on the circle's upper right edge. The final product ought to resemble an egg in shape. In this instance, the chicken comes after the egg!

To serve as a guide for the head, draw another circle above the torso on the right side. Because roosters have tiny heads, make the circle small. Avoid setting the circle too high to avoid giving your rooster a lengthy neck.

As a guide for the beak, draw a triangle-like shape on the right side of the rooster's head.

To create the neck, draw a few lines that join the rooster's head and body.

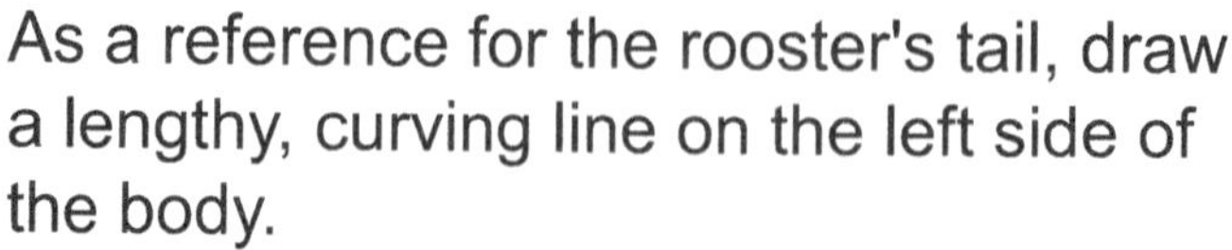

As a reference for the rooster's tail, draw a lengthy, curving line on the left side of the body.

As a reference for the rooster's feet, draw an L-shaped line beneath the torso.

On the top of the rooster's head, softly sketch a circle to serve as the eye. The circle should then be made darker and the top portion flatter to resemble a half-circle more. Except for a little circle to depict glare, the inside of the eye should be shaded. In order to get the pupil's darker value, apply more pressure with your pencil close to the center of the eye. For added detail, add a few lines around the rooster's eye.

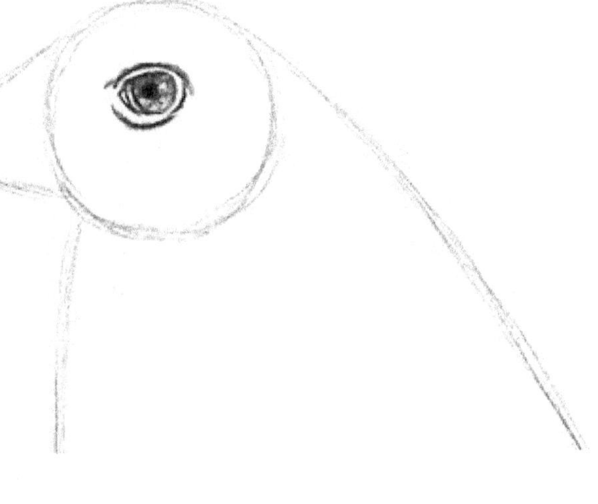

Draw the rooster's beak using the triangular shape as a guidance. For the mouth, draw a curved line close to the triangle's center. The beak's top and bottom pieces should be added after that, with the tip pointing slightly downward. For the rooster's nose, draw a tiny oval at the top.

On the rooster's head, draw a crest or comb. First, create the two curved lines that will be the comb's sides. To complete the comb, insert the curved spikes between the sides. Draw each spike with a varying thickness and length, the longer ones in the center.

Using the original circle as a reference, draw the remainder of the rooster's head. For the fleshy area inside the rooster's head, draw a line around its eye. Add a few shorter strokes below the eye for the detail inside the head.

Draw the rooster's feet using the L-shaped line at the bottom as a reference. As you trace the line's route, lightly draw the leg's shape. Three of a rooster's toes point forward, and one points backward. On the leg, it also has a spur higher up. Darken the lines once you get the rooster's foot structure correct. If you'd like, you can lengthen the spur on the foot. Include the talons on the tips of the toes as well. Then, using the first foot as a guide, draw the rooster's foot on the other side. To ensure the proper structure, first lightly sketch the form of the foot. Then add the rooster's toes and darken the lines.

Use the initial forms as a reference as you draw the first portion of the rooster's body. Draw a curving line for the feathers that overlap and drape over the wing on the left side of the first circle. For the fine details of the feathers in the rear, make short, rapid strokes inside that form.

Draw a succession of lines to represent the rooster's folded wing inside the original circle on the lower right side. Draw the lines in the same direction as the feathers using short, swift strokes. At the top of the circle, the lines should be thin, and as they descend, they should progressively become thicker.

The lines that join the rooster's head to its body should be made darker to represent the neck. The lower portion of the neck feathers should be drawn with brief, swift strokes. For the neck detail, add some strokes inside as well.

The rooster's lengthy tail feathers should be drawn using the curved line on the left side as a guide. Be remember to stop the movie so you may sketch the rooster at your own leisure because drawing the tail feathers can be challenging. For the first tail feather, draw a lengthy, curving arc close to the center of the initial line. Then, at the top of the guiding line, draw two feathers that are even longer and overlap one another. Add a feather between these two, one under the first middle feather, and one beneath the top two. After drawing the initial guide line for the foundation feathers, add a few feathers close to its bottom. You're not required to have exactly the same feathers.

As much of the initial guide lines as you can remove for a cleaner appearance. Concerning removing them all, don't worry. You can abandon some of them. Redraw any lines from the final sketch that you might have inadvertently removed.

To give your rooster drawing additional depth and volume, add some shading. When shading, choose the light source's direction so that the shadows follow it. To obtain varying levels of tonal value, alter the pressure you apply to your pencil.

The front of the sea turtle's shell should be drawn using a circle as a guide. The circle need not be flawless. It is merely a guide.

To complete the guidance for the sea turtle's shell, draw a lengthy arc on the circle's left side. The arc's length should be a little bit longer than the circle's diameter.

On the right side of the shell, trace a little oval to serve as a guide for the sea turtle's head. The oval should be roughly one-third the diameter of the circle at the start. Avoid moving the oval too much to the right to avoid having an excessively lengthy neck for the turtle.

Draw two lines that cross one another inside the circle. You can later use these lines to help you identify the sea turtle's facial traits.

The sea turtle's neck is shown by two brief, curving lines that link the head and shell.

As guidance for the feet that resemble flippers, draw a few arcs beneath the sea turtle's torso. The flippers should be shaped like a U with a diagonal orientation. Affix the rear one close to the shell's tip and the front one under the neck.

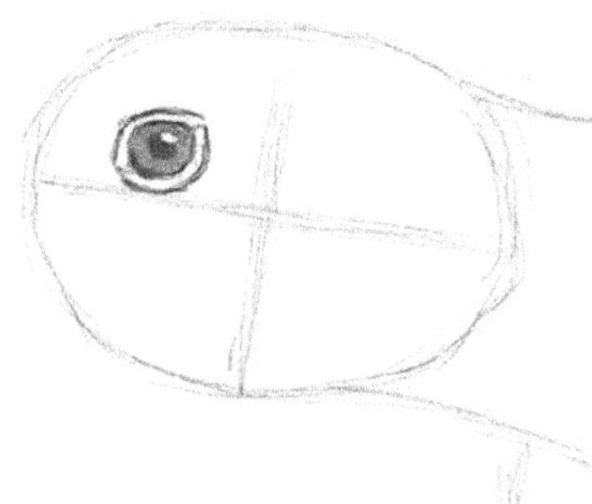

Use the lines as a reference to draw the sea turtle's eye as a little oval on the top right side of the head. Make a little circle within the eye to indicate the glare. For the pupil, create a second circle and shade it in. Use a value that is lighter than the pupil to shade in the remaining areas of the sea turtle's eye. To add more detail, add a few lines around the eye.

Use the front of the oval as a guide to draw the mouth. Under each eye, draw a curved line that reaches toward the interior of the mouth's oval shape. To make the top of the sea turtle's mouth, trace the original oval's outline. For the chin, add a second curving line beneath the lips.

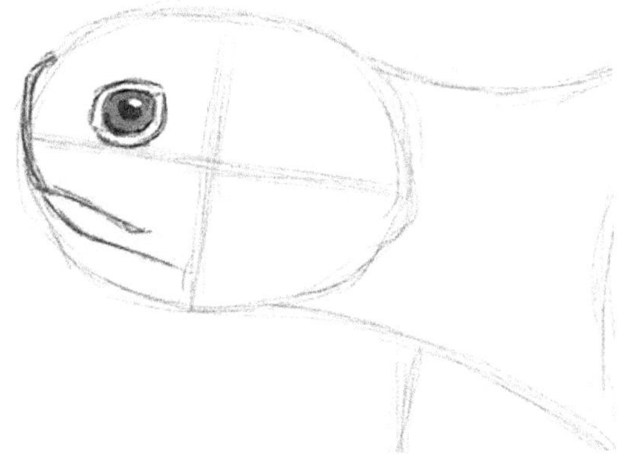

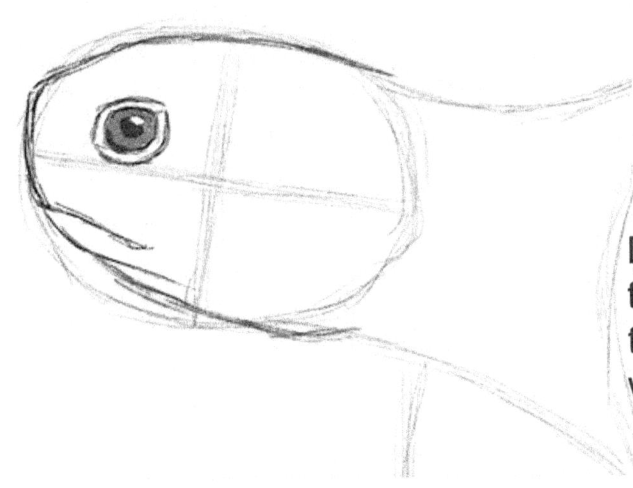

Draw the rest of the sea turtle's head using the initial oval as a reference. Darken the line that forms the top and bottom of the head while following the oval's trajectory.

Draw the sea turtle's front flipper using the arc on the right as a reference. Follow the fundamental arc's route as you quickly sketch up the flipper's shape. Darken the lines once the framework is perfect. More curved on the right side, it joins the shell near the top. A wavy line makes up the left side.

Using the basic forms as a reference, draw the upper half of the sea turtle's shell. The top of the shell is made by drawing a line along the original circle's and the arc's path. By lightly drawing a lengthy line over both shapes, create the bottom portion. The original shapes do not meet in the middle where the top and bottom shells should. The bottom of the line is getting closer. As you darken the bottom, draw little, slightly arced lines rather than one large, curved line.

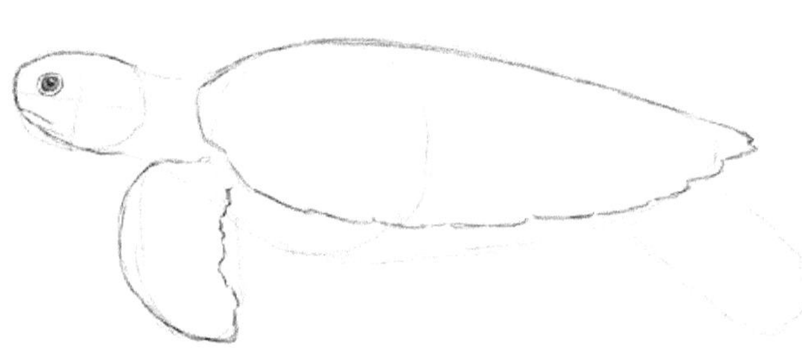

On the top of the sea turtle's shell, trace the pentagonal shapes. For structure, begin by lightly drawing several pointed lines at the top and a long curving line near the bottom. Darken the lines after you've softly sketched the fundamental pattern. Wide letter V-shaped lines make up the bottom of the shapes. The pentagon-like shapes in the center can now be made by drawing vertical lines. The lines begin at the tips of the upper shapes and stop at the bottom, where a thin line has been softly sketched. Create the little shapes along the border of the top shell by drawing a succession of brief lines along the bottom. It can be a little challenging to draw the shapes on the shell,

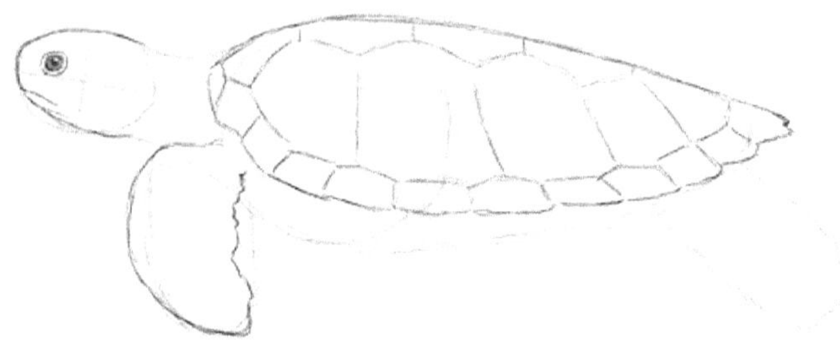

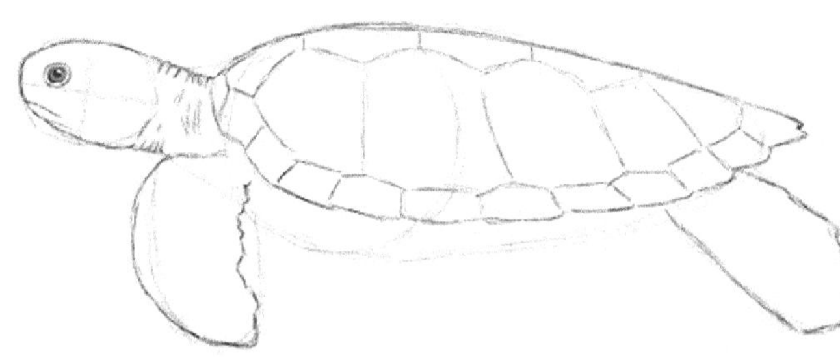

To draw the neck, follow the lines that connect the shell with the head. For the wrinkly skin, make a series of short, closely spaced lines on the top, bottom, and middle of the neck. The sea turtle's hind flipper should be drawn using the left side's arc as a guide. As you adhere to the fundamental arc's course, make the left side of the flipper waver.

Create the lowest portion of the sea turtle's shell by darkening the bottom line.

For the visible area of the flippers on the other side, draw a few lines behind the front and back flippers.

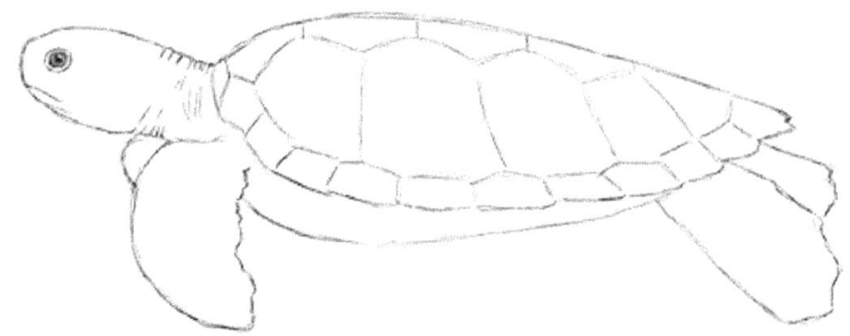

Erase as much of the initial guiding lines as you can for a cleaner appearance. Don't stress about removing every guide. You can abandon some of them. Redraw any lines from the final sketch that you might have inadvertently removed.

To give your sea turtle drawing additional depth and substance, add some shading. When shading, choose the light source's direction so that the shadows follow it. To obtain varying levels of tonal value, alter the pressure you apply to your pencil.

To make your sea turtle drawing more full, you can add more details. Draw shapes of varying sizes across its skin and tone them in since green sea turtles have large, black scales on their bodies. If you don't want to add the scales since doing so would take too much time, you can simply add solid values all over the body.

How to Draw a **Shark**

As a guide, sketch a long, slender oval for the body of the great white shark.

As a reference for the shark's head, draw an angled line that resembles an arrow on the left side of the oval.

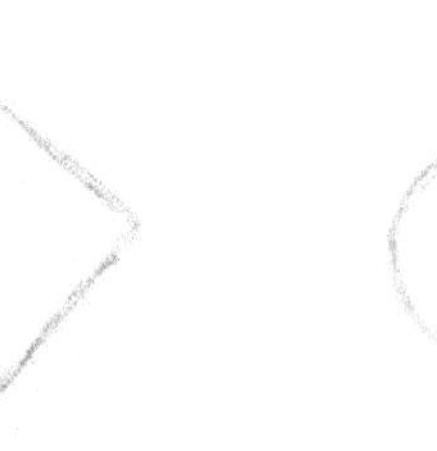

On the side of the oval opposite the oval, draw a triangle with a left-pointing triangle for the shark's caudal fin or tail.

Connect the shark's body and
caudal fin with a few lines.

Draw the dorsal and pectoral fins of the
great white shark, which are essentially
triangles at the top and bottom of the oval.

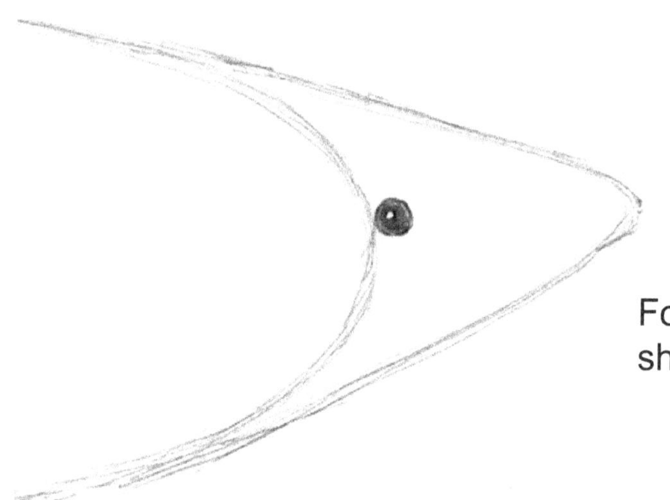

For the shark's eye, create a little circle and
shade it in on the left side of the oval.

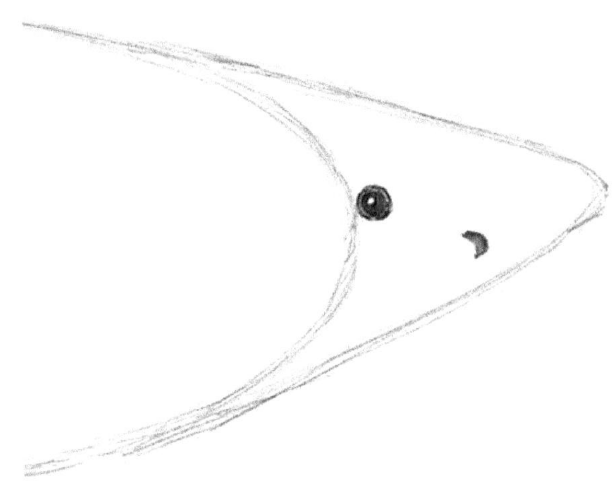

For the great white shark's nose, draw a thin, curving line beneath and to the left of the eye.

Make a mouth and head for the shark. Create the lips by sloping the line toward the right as you draw the head. Include the lower jaw with the little triangles that make up the teeth.

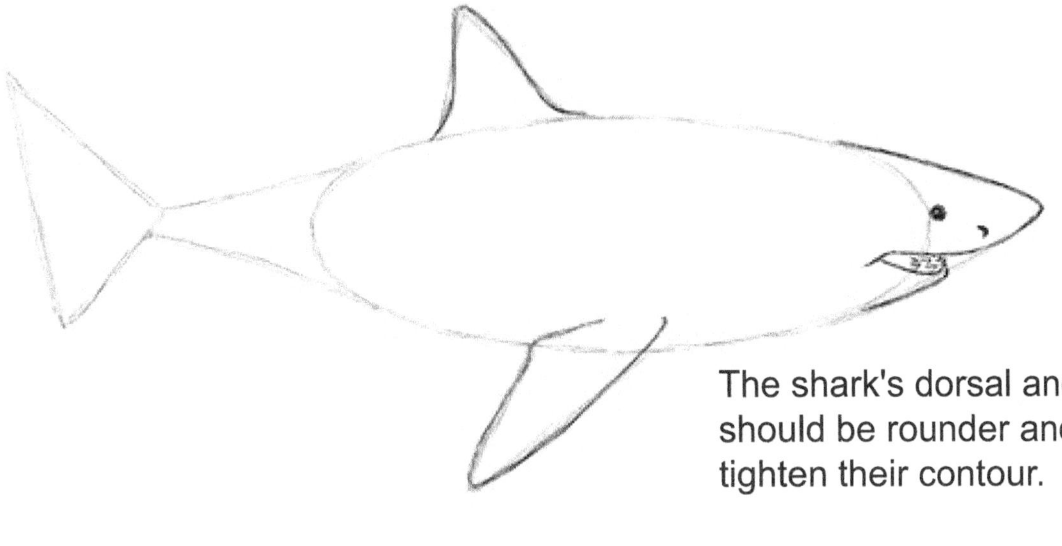

The shark's dorsal and pectoral fins should be rounder and darker as you tighten their contour.

Tighten the shark's caudal fin as well, using the triangle as a reference. Make sure the middle dips inward.

Include the pelvic fins, anal, and second dorsal of the shark in your drawing. These have rounded tops and resemble little triangles.

Darken the remainder of the great white shark's body, using the primary oval as a guide.

Draw a few vertical lines for the shark's gills on the upper, left side of the pectoral fin.

To depict the countershading of the shark, draw a line across the body of the great white shark (the split in color from the top and bottom).

As much of the first guiding lines as you can remove for a cleaner appearance. Concerning removing them all, don't worry. You can abandon some of them.

To give your great white shark drawing additional depth and substance, add some shading. When shading, choose the light source's direction so that the shadows follow it. To get different levels of tonal value, alter the pressure you apply to your pencil.

Since great white sharks are actually gray, you can give your drawing a darker hue to add additional realism. Using references can help you be as accurate as you can. To imitate underwater sheen, you can leave a section near the top of the body unshadowed.